Sports Illustrated KIDS

STARS OF SPORTS

ZION WILLIAMSON

BASKETBALL'S RISING STAR

▪▮▮ by Matt Chandler

CAPSTONE PRESS
a capstone imprint

Stars of Sports is published by Capstone Press, an imprint of Capstone.
1710 Roe Crest Drive,
North Mankato, Minnesota 56003
www.capstonepub.com

Library of Congress Cataloging-in-Publication Data
Names: Chandler, Matt, author.
Title: Zion Williamson : basketball's rising star / by Matt Chandler.
Description: North Mankato : Capstone Press, a Capstone imprint, [2021] | Series: Sports
    illustrated kids stars of sports | Includes bibliographical references and index. | Audience:
Ages 8–11 | Audience: Grades 4–6
Identifiers: LCCN 2020037784 (print) | LCCN 2020037785 (ebook) | ISBN 9781496695314
    (hardcover) | ISBN 9781977155498 (eBook PDF) | ISBN 9781977157119 (kindle edition)
Subjects: LCSH: Williamson, Zion, 2000– —Juvenile literature. | Basketball players—United
    States—Biography—Juvenile literature.
Classification: LCC GV884.W585 C43 2021 (print) | LCC GV884.W585 (ebook) |
    DDC 796.323092 [B]—dc23
LC record available at https://lccn.loc.gov/2020037784
LC ebook record available at https://lccn.loc.gov/2020037785

Summary: Zion Williamson was a record-breaking high school athlete in South Carolina.
He went on to lead Duke University's basketball team in scoring and rebounding. Williamson's
outstanding performance made him the number one pick in the 2019 NBA Draft. Though
his 2019 season started with an injury and ended with a pandemic, his future is bright. Learn
about Williamson's steady climb to the top and find out where he wants to go from there.

Editorial Credits
Editor, Mandy Robbins; Designers: Elyse White and Lori Bye; Media Researcher: Eric Gohl;
Production Specialist: Spencer Rosio

Photo Credits
AP Photo: Craig Mitchelldyer, Cover, Gregory Payan, 10, Mark Lennihan, 19, Nam Y. Huh,
28; Getty Images: Raleigh News & Observer, 13; Newscom: Adriana M. Barraza/WENN.
com, 7, Ethan Hyman/Raleigh News & Observer, 15, Jevone Moore/Icon Sportswire DMK,
5, Kyodo, 17, 18, Patrick Schneider/Charlotte Observer, bottom left 25, Ringo Chiu/ZUMA
Wire, top left 25, Robin Alam/Icon Sportswire, 12, Stephen Lew/Icon Sportswire, 21, 23,
middle right 25, 26, Tracy Glantz/The State/TNS, 9; Shutterstock: EFKS, 1

All internet sites appearing in back matter were available and accurate when this book was
sent to press.

Direct Quotations
Page 6: from "'My Mom Is the Hardest Coach I've Ever Had,' Says Zion Williamson," by John
    Lynch, CNN, April 28, 2020, https://www.cnn.com/2020/04/28/sport/zion-williamson-nba-
    twitter-interview-spt-intl/index.html.
Page 16: from "Zion Williamson on if drafted by Knicks: 'I would love to play for them'," by
    Adam Zagoria, SportsNet New York, April 5, 2019, https://www.sny.tv/articles/zion-
    williamson-on-if-drafted-by-knicks-i-would-love-to-play-for-them
Page 19: from "Zion Williamson gets emotional after New Orleans Pelicans select him No. 1
    overall,"ESPN, June 20, 2019, https://www.youtube.com/watch?v=eMidlVTaubY.
Page 27: from "Former Duke men's basketball star Zion Williamson pledges to pay salary for
    Pelicans workers," by Evan Kolin, The Chronicle, March 13, 2020, https://www.
    dukechronicle.com/article/2020/03/former-duke-mens-basketball-star-zion-williamson-
    pledges-to-pay-salary-for-pelicans-workers.

TABLE OF CONTENTS

Glossary terms are **BOLD** on first use.

ROCKIN' ROOKIE

New Orleans Pelicans' fans had waited seven long months for this moment. The announcer introduced Zion Williamson. He jogged onto the court in a red Pelicans warm-up suit. Fans cheered wildly!

Williamson had missed half the season with a knee injury. But on January 22, 2020, he was finally ready to make his National Basketball Association (NBA) **debut**. It took until early in the second quarter for Williamson to score his first points. Teammate Nickeil Alexander-Walker shot a jumper but missed. Williamson went up for the rebound. He took two quick dribbles and took a shot off the backboard to score his first official NBA basket!

<<< Williamso'ns 22-point performance was one of the best ever by a rookie playing his first game in the NBA.

Williamson was just getting started. He scored 17 straight points for the Pelicans. New Orleans lost the game. But Williamson finished tied for the team lead with 22 points.

CHAPTER ONE

BORN TO BALL

Zion Williamson was born in Salisbury, North Carolina, on July 6, 2000. He came from a family of athletes. His mom, Sharonda Sampson, was a track star in college. His father, Lateef Williamson, played football for Livingstone College.

Williamson's parents divorced when he was five years old. Sampson married a man named Lee Anderson. Anderson had played basketball at Clemson University. Anderson was an **Amateur Athletic Union** (AAU) coach.

With his parents' athletic backgrounds, Williamson seemed **destined** to be an athlete. They built Williamson into a young basketball star.

"My stepfather and my mother would just say, 'If you want to be one of the greatest, you've got to work when nobody's working," Williamson once said.

<<< Williamson (center) won the 2019 ESPY Award for Best College Athlete. He attended the ceremony with his family.

FACT

Zion was named after Mount Zion. It is the highest point in Jerusalem, Israel.

HIGH SCHOOL HEROICS

Williamson's parents sent him to Spartanburg Day School. It is a small private high school in South Carolina. In eighth grade, Williamson was 5 feet 10 inches (178 centimeters) tall. But in two years, he grew to be 6 feet 6 inches (198 cm). His tenth grade year, Williamson led the Spartanburg Day School Griffins to its first State Championship. He averaged 28 points and 10 rebounds per game for the 2015–16 season.

Williamson returned for his junior year hoping to be even better. By then he was famous. His dunks were being shown on ESPN. When his team played in a tournament, the games sold out. People wanted to see the young man who some were comparing to superstar NBA player LeBron James.

Williamson delivered once again the following year. He led the Griffins to their second straight state title. Williamson scored 51 of his team's 76 points!

>>> Williamson became famous for his big-time dunks against opposing teams during his high school years.

>>> Williamson's skills on the court grew stronger as he led his high school team to three straight state championships.

SENIOR STAR

By the time he was a senior in 2018, Williamson was one of the top **recruits** in the nation. Top college coaches were watching his games. Many experts already believed Williamson would play only one season at the college level and then move on to the NBA. He was seen as a top pick in the 2019 NBA Draft.

Still, the teenager stayed focused on his final high school season. He wanted to win a third state title. With his team ahead in the second half of the championship game, Williamson put on a show. He delivered a windmill dunk that wowed the crowd. He threw down a reverse dunk as well. Williamson ended the game with 37 points and 17 rebounds. His team easily won their third state title.

FACT

When he was five years old, Williamson told his stepfather his dream was to play basketball at Duke.

CHAPTER TWO

DUKE SUPERSTAR

Williamson received more than a dozen **scholarship** offers. In the end, he went with Duke University in North Carolina. Williamson would get to learn under coach Mike Krzyzewski. "Coach K" had led the Duke Blue Devils to five national championships at that point.

Most fans were sure Williamson would only play one season at Duke before entering the NBA Draft. They hoped he could deliver the Blue Devils a national title.

>>> Mike Krzyzewski (right) has won more games than any coach in college basketball history.

As a college freshman, Williamson was a great player. He started in 33 of the Blue Devils' 38 games. Williamson averaged 22.6 points and 8.9 rebounds per game. He led the Blue Devils to the Atlantic Coast Conference (ACC) Championship. He was named the tournament's most valuable player (MVP).

Shoe Explosion

Williamson's Blue Devils were taking on the University of North Carolina on February 20, 2019. Williamson took a pass and cut toward the top of the **key**. Suddenly, he fell to the floor, grabbing his knee. When Williamson cut, his Nike shoe had ripped open. His entire foot came out! Williamson suffered a sprained knee. Nike **stock** lost more than $1 billion the next day.

TOURNAMENT KING

Expectations were high for the Blue Devils entering the 2019 National Collegiate Athletic Association (NCAA) Tournament. They were favored to win the national title. In three out of four tournament games, Williamson led the team in scoring. He became the first **rookie** to top 100 points in the NCAA Tournament since Derrick Rose in 2008.

But it wasn't enough. The Blue Devils' impressive season came to an end against Michigan State in the East Regional Finals. Williamson played well. He led the team with 24 points and 14 rebounds. But he came up one basket short as the Blue Devils fell 68–67 to the Spartans.

FACT

Williamson was so popular, the TV network airing the NCAA tournament had a "Zion Cam." It followed him for every minute of every tournament game.

>>> During the 2019 NCAA Basketball Tournament, Williamson averaged 26 points and 8.5 rebounds per game.

CHAPTER THREE

DRAFT MANIA

There was no real drama about who the number-one pick would be in the 2019 NBA Draft. Anyone who knew anything about basketball was sure it would be Williamson.

The 2019 NBA Draft **Lottery** was set for May 14, 2019. There had been **speculation** that Williamson wanted to play in a big-market city such as New York. Some experts thought he would refuse to sign a contract with any other team. They thought Williamson would try to force a trade to the New York Knicks if they didn't win the lottery.

But when asked about his options, Williamson answered the question perfectly. "Whatever NBA team I land on, that's where I want to be," he said.

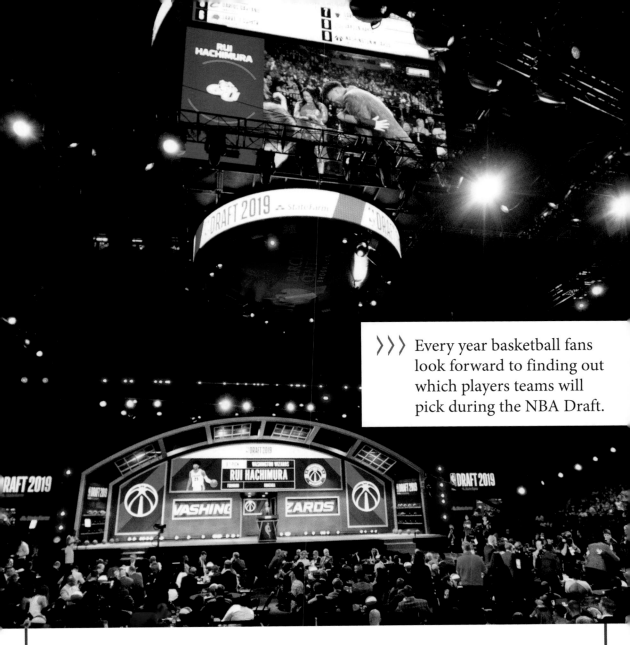

> ⟩⟩⟩ Every year basketball fans look forward to finding out which players teams will pick during the NBA Draft.

In the end, the New Orleans Pelicans won the top pick. As soon as the Pelicans won the draft lottery, they sold more than 3,000 season tickets. Everyone assumed they'd pick Williamson. Pelicans fans couldn't wait to see him play for their team.

DRAFT DAY

On draft day, NBA Commissioner Adam Silver read Williamson's name as the first draft pick. Williamson rose from his seat. He hugged his mom and stepdad. They are the two people he credits most with his success.

》》》 Williamson poses for photos with NBA Commissioner Adam Silver after being picked number one overall in the 2019 NBA Draft.

Williamson walked across the stage in a white suit with a big smile on his face. He pulled on a New Orleans Pelicans cap. The crowd cheered as he smiled and posed for photos. He used this opportunity as a chance to thank his mother.

"I didn't think I'd be in this position," he told the crowd. *"My mom sacrificed a lot for me. I wouldn't be here without my mom."*

>>> Williamson spoke to reporters about his dream of becoming a pro player before the 2019 NBA Draft.

CHAPTER FOUR

PELICAN POWER

Williamson looked strong in the NBA Summer League. He averaged 23 points per game in the preseason. He also led the team in rebounds and steals.

Williamson was less than a week from making his NBA debut when disaster struck. He went down with a knee injury during a preseason game. It was the same knee he had hurt at Duke. The Pelicans expected their new star to miss a few weeks. Instead, it took Williamson three months to recover.

It was the fourth knee injury the 19-year-old Williamson had suffered in his career. It made fans wonder if he would be able to stay healthy long enough to bring the Pelicans an NBA Championship.

>>> Williamson had to start the 2019 season on the injured list. But he still worked to encourage his Pelicans teammates on the sideline.

DAZZLING DEBUT

Williamson's injury meant he missed the Pelicans' first 44 games. But basketball fans eventually got to see him play. He started 19 games before the coronavirus **pandemic** cut the 2019–20 season short. Williamson averaged 22.5 points per game his first season. While he was injured, the Pelicans went 17–27. But in the 24 games he played that season, the team was 12–12.

Williamson's best game as a pro came at home. It was against the Los Angeles Lakers and LeBron James. Williamson outscored James 35–34. But James came back with the game on the line. The Lakers held a two-point lead with two and a half minutes left. Williamson was guarding James when the Lakers' star took a three-point shot. James's basket sealed the Lakers' win.

FACT

Williamson became the first rookie player to score 20 or more points in seven straight games since Carmelo Anthony in 2004.

〉〉〉 Williamson (right) puts up a shot against Los Angeles Lakers forward Kyle Kuzma during a home game at Smoothie King Center in New Orleans, Louisiana.

CHAPTER FIVE

FUTURE SUPERSTAR?

Williamson has been compared to Michael Jordan and LeBron James since he was in high school. It is too soon to tell how he will grow as a player. But is it possible he could earn a place alongside the all-time greats? Williamson has shown early on that his talent matches the greatest players in the game.

Williamson played 24 games in his first season. He topped 20 points in 19 of those games. Through his first 24 games, Jordan had 20 games scoring 20 or more points. James put up 20 or more in just nine of his first 24 NBA games.

Williamson compares well in rebounds too. Through 24 games, James piled up 152 rebounds, Williamson, 150, and Jordan 123.

LeBron James
Scored 20+ points in
first 24 games: 6 times

Michael Jordan
Scored 20+ points in
first 24 games: 15 times

Zion Williamson
Scored 20+ points in
first 24 games: 19 times

OFF-COURT SUPERSTAR

In today's NBA, playing the game is only one part of being an athlete. Players have the chance to make more money off the court than they do on it. In 2019, Williamson signed a $75 million shoe deal with Jordan Brand before ever playing an NBA game. He also signed big deals with 2K Sports, Gatorade, and Mountain Dew.

>>> Williamson's skills on the court have helped him become a leader both in the NBA and in his community.

Williamson's off-court roles also allow him to make a difference in his community. He worked with Mountain Dew to rebuild two basketball courts near Spartanburg Day School. The courts are painted with fun cartoon images of Williamson as a superhero dunking the basketball!

Giving Back

When a pandemic shut down the NBA in 2020, Williamson stepped up. The workers at the Pelicans' arena were out of jobs. Williamson volunteered to pay their salaries for the first month of the shutdown. "My mother has always set an example for me about being respectful for others and being grateful for what we have," Williamson said on Instagram. "This is a small way for me to express my support and appreciation for these wonderful people . . ."

FUTURE POTENTIAL

Coming out of Duke, many people had already crowned Williamson a future Hall of Fame player. The question remains—how good can he be? Williamson hasn't had the chance to live up to the high expectations fans have.

Do you think he has what it takes to be one of the all-time greats? His first games in the NBA showed he might. Only time will tell if he will continue to improve and lead the NBA for years to come.

>>> Williamson goes up for a dramatic dunk shot during the NBA Rising Stars game on February 14, 2020.

TIMELINE

2000 Zion Lateef Williamson is born in Salisbury, North Carolina, on July 6.

2016 Williamson is named MVP of the Under Armour Elite 24 All-Star Game.

2018 Williamson graduates from Spartanburg Day School.

2018 Williamson announces he will play for Duke University.

2018 On November 6, Williamson plays his first game with Duke, scoring 28 points to beat rival Kentucky.

2019 The New Orleans Pelicans select Williamson with the first pick in the NBA Draft on June 20.

2019 In July, Williamson signs a four-year contract with the Pelicans worth as much as $45 million. He also signed a five-year, $75-million sneaker deal with Jordan Brand.

2020 Williamson makes his NBA debut on January 22 and scores 22 points.

GLOSSARY

AMATEUR (AM-uh-chur)—an athlete who is not paid for playing a sport

AMATEUR ATHLETIC UNION (AM-uh-chur ath-LEH-tik YOO-yun)—a national organization dedicated to promoting amateur sports

DEBUT (day-BYOO)—a player's first game

DESTINED (DES-tind)—foretold to happen or meant to be

KEY (KEE)—the painted area under the basket; also known as the "lane"

LOTTERY (LOT-ur-ee)—a way of randomly choosing someone to win a prize or participate in an event

PANDEMIC (pan-DEM-ik)—an epidemic that spreads throughout the world and infects many people at once

RECRUIT (ri-KROOT)—a player that a team seeks out to join them

ROOKIE (RUK-ee)—a first-year player

SCHOLARSHIP (SKOL-ur-ship)—money given to a student to pay for school

SPECULATION (spek-yoo-LAY-shuhn)—ideas about what might happen

STOCK (STOK)—the value of a company, divided into shares when sold to investors

READ MORE

Bryant, Howard. *Legends: The Best Players, Games and Teams in Basketball.* New York: Philomel Books, 2017.

Chandler, Matt. *Pro Basketball Records: A Guide for Every Fan.* North Mankato, MN: Compass Point Books, 2019.

Smith, Elliott. *Zion Williamson.* Minneapolis: Lerner Publications, 2021.

INTERNET SITES

Zion Williamson's Career Stats
basketball-reference.com/players/w/willizi01.html

New Orleans Pelicans Official Website
nba.com/pelicans/

Zion Williamson Biography
espn.com/nba/player/_/id/4395628/zion-williamson

INDEX